Table of Contents

Introduction i
Why This Book iii

The Beginning: "Medicare Stress Defined" 1
- Why Is Medicare So Stressful? 1
- Factor #1: Lack of Experience 1
- Factor #2: Excessive Mail 2
- Factor #3: Phone Calls (Excessive and Aggressive) 3
- Factor #4: Door-to-Door Sales 3
- Factor #5: Misinformation 4
- Factor #6: Medicare Parts versus Medicare Plans 4
- Moving Ahead 5
- Stress-Reducing Actions 5

Action #1: Sign up for the National Do Not Call Registry 7

Action #2: Create a Filing System with Four Folders 9

Action #3: Avoid Online Quoting 11

Action #4: Learn About Medicare 13
- What Is Medicare? 13
- Medicare Eligibility 14
- How to Sign Up for Medicare 14
- When to Sign Up for Medicare 14
- What If You Miss Your Initial Enrollment Period? 15
- What If You Want to Keep Your Employer Insurance? 16

- Employee Insurance and Medicare Part B 16
- Avoiding Penalties 17
- Medicare Enrollment Review 17
- Original Medicare (Parts A & B) 18
- Original Medicare Card 18
- Original Medicare Part A: Coverage, Costs, and Copays.... 19
- Original Medicare Part B: Coverage, Costs, and Copays.... 20
- What Is Not Covered by Original Medicare Parts A and B? 21
- Financial Risks of Original Medicare 22
- Medicare A and B Section Review 22

Action #5: Learn about Medicare Insurance Products 24
- Medicare Supplements 24
- Standardized Plans 25
- Benefit Structures 25
- Medicare Supplement Premiums 26
- Eliminating Financial Risk 26
- Practical Application 27
- National Coverage 27
- Important Questions 28
- Medicare Supplement Review 28
- Part D (Prescription Drug Plans) 29
- How to Obtain Part D Coverage 29
- Medication Tiers 30
- Part D Phases 30
- Monthly Premiums 32
- Deductible or No Deductible 32
- Formularies 33
- Preferred or Standard Pharmacies 33
- Important Questions 33
- Medicare Part D Review 34
- Medicare Advantage Plans (Part C) 34
- HMOs or PPOs 35
- How Medicare Advantage Plans Function 36
- Out-of-Pocket Maximums 37

Medicare
Stress Relief

A clear plan for transitioning to Medicare and reducing *STRESS*.

William A. Simmons, CPA

outskirts
press

Medicare Stress Relief
All Rights Reserved.
Copyright © 2022 William A. Simmons, CPA
v3.0

The opinions expressed in this manuscript are solely the opinions of the author and do not represent the opinions or thoughts of the publisher. The author has represented and warranted full ownership and/or legal right to publish all the materials in this book.

This book may not be reproduced, transmitted, or stored in whole or in part by any means, including graphic, electronic, or mechanical without the express written consent of the publisher except in the case of brief quotations embodied in critical articles and reviews.

Outskirts Press, Inc.
http://www.outskirtspress.com

ISBN: 978-1-9772-5248-7

Cover Photo © 2022 www.gettyimages.com. All rights reserved - used with permission.

Outskirts Press and the "OP" logo are trademarks belonging to Outskirts Press, Inc.

PRINTED IN THE UNITED STATES OF AMERICA

- Prescription Coverage or No Prescription Coverage 37
- High-Risk Areas 38
- Premiums 39
- Additional Benefits 39
- Pre-Existing Conditions 39
- Important Questions 40
- Medicare Advantage Plan Review 41
- Indemnity Plans 41
- Cancer Indemnity Policy Example 42
- Hospital Indemnity Policy Example 42
- Indemnity Plan Review 42

Action #6: Select a Medicare Product 43
- Section A Questions 43
- Section B Questions 44

Action #7: Identify Plan Options Available in Your Area 45
- Steps for Identifying Medicare Advantage Plans 46
- Steps for Identifying Prescription Drug Plans 47
- Steps for Identifying Medicare Supplement Plans 48

Action #8: Contact an Agent and Schedule an Appointment 50
- Agent Options 50
- Agent Recommendations 51
- Finding Agents 52

Action #9: Meet with Agent and Enroll in a Plan 54

Conclusion 56

Introduction

First let me say, "I love what I do." I never imagined when graduating from college that I would be a Medicare insurance specialist. I remember telling my best friend and college roommate after coming back from an interview with a large insurance company, "I don't want to be an insurance agent." Well, after more than twenty years as a licensed CPA and six years of experience as a chaplain, guess what? I am a licensed insurance agent! Over the last seven years, I have worked with hundreds of individuals who have transitioned to Medicare from employer insurance plans and other insurance options. I can say this with complete confidence. Only a few people I have met had a good understanding of Medicare.

Almost everyone I have met with had some level of stress, confusion, or uncertainty regarding Medicare decisions, which is how I define <u>Medicare stress</u>. Unfortunately, I do not expect the stress and confusion surrounding Medicare to magically go away. Why, because the intense competition for customers has created a stressful environment. I wish it were not the case. However, the stress and confusion created by the marketing of Medicare is the origin of this book. I trust that if you read this book, it will help you manage your transition to Medicare and relieve some of your stress.

Why This Book

I published *Medicare & The Stress of Turning 65* in 2020. I believe it <u>was</u> and <u>is</u> still a good book. However, I am driven to improve upon my efforts. That is why I have revised and renamed the book *Medicare Stress Relief*. Turning sixty-five and becoming eligible for Medicare is going to create stress for most people. However, it's not only individuals who are turning sixty-five that experience Medicare stress. It can be anyone eligible or currently enrolled in Medicare that can experience <u>Medicare Stress</u>. The question becomes, "How are you going to handle this stress?"

There are a lot of books about Medicare and information abounds regarding Medicare insurance products. What is not out there is a book that teaches you how to manage your transition to Medicare and minimize the stress you experience during the process. That is what I am presenting in this book.

Simply put, *Medicare Stress Relief* is my recommended action plan if you want to stop feeling overwhelmed, confused, or uncertain about your knowledge of Medicare or what you can do to make your Medicare transition less stressful. There is no magic bullet to solve your Medicare stress; however, if you spend a few hours following the <u>actions</u> I suggest, you can take charge of your Medicare transition. Although it may seem like everywhere you turn, someone is attempting to sell you Medicare insurance products, my hope for this book is to help you prepare for the process.

The Beginning: "Medicare Stress Defined"

<u>Medicare stress</u> is defined as any feelings of being overwhelmed, confused, or uncertain about Medicare insurance decisions. These feelings are usually caused by a lack of understanding or knowledge about Medicare and/or external pressures from insurance companies, marketing organizations, or sales agents.

Why Is Medicare So Stressful?

Several factors contribute to the stress created when you become eligible for Medicare. First, you are forced into a decision about an insurance option of which you have no experience. Second, you have become the focus or target of every insurance company that sells Medicare insurance products. This manifests itself in excessive amounts of mail and probably unwanted phone calls.

Also, if you are one of the lucky ones, you may have a salesperson knocking on your door attempting to sell you insurance. Thirdly, you will have to deal with a large amount of misinformation about Medicare from family, friends, or acquaintances. Once you Combine your lack of experience with external pressures and Medicare misinformation, you have a recipe for stress and confusion. Just know one thing, it's not your fault! There are several forces and factors at work that are outside of your control.

Factor #1: Lack of Experience

The first reason becoming eligible for Medicare causes stress is that you are dealing with a new subject. If you are like most people, you have had minimal, if any, experience with Medicare. Maybe you have heard a friend or relative talk about it, but chances are you have not spent much time reading or learning about it. Frankly, most individuals know of Medicare, but do not know a lot about Medicare

Imagine yourself as a teenager and being asked to take your driving exam without any warning or preparation. It would have created a lot of anxiety. Dealing with Medicare is similar. If you have little knowledge or experience, it is going to create stress. For most people, dealing with new experiences creates some level of apprehension. It's no different dealing with Medicare. It is a new experience, which will bring about some anxiety.

Factor #2: Excessive Mail

Holy cow! You will not believe the excessive amount of mail you will receive (if not already). If you are not familiar with Medicare products, deciding what information to keep and what to throw away can create stress. I will help you with this issue as we move forward. At this point, I want to share with you the types of mail you may receive.

The first type of mail is marketing directly from insurance companies. This information is identified by company names and logos, etc. It can be helpful. It can also create confusion if the company offers several Medicare products.

The second type of mail is classified as Business Replay Mail. This mail is sent from several different sources. This mail attempts to get you to respond by calling a 1-800 number or by returning a card with your contact information. It will often come with headlines such as "Get more benefits" or "Did you know you could be receiving this benefit?" This mail is designed to entice you into a reply. Be careful! If you send in a reply card with your phone number, there is usually some fine print that gives the sender permission to contact you.

You may also receive Business Reply Mail from companies that are attempting to generate leads. If you respond to this mail with your personal information, your information is then sold to agents or other marketing organizations. I recommend that you do not respond to Business Reply Mail from out-of-state addresses or any that include a 1-800 number. You want to avoid opening that can of worms.

Lastly, you will get mail from local agents. In many cases, the local agents will be promoting their services. In some cases, you will have local agents promoting Medicare education classes. Whether you attend their classes or not, I encourage you to keep the information from the local agents. If you follow the guidance I provide later in the book, you will need the local agent's information.

Regardless of the source, you will receive an excessive amount of mail. You may decide to throw it away or stack it on your kitchen table. <u>In Action #2, I will suggest how you can use the mail to your advantage.</u>

Factor #3: Phone Calls (Excessive and Aggressive)

Most of my clients tell me phone calls from insurance companies and sales agents usually start about three to four months before they turn sixty-five. Unfortunately, the calls can become excessive. There is some irony that a major source of your <u>Medicare stress</u> will be from people who want to **help** you. Some telemarketing tactics can be aggressive. For example, some telemarketing agents will attempt to scare you into enrolling by talking about Medicare penalties. Another tactic is when an agent pushes you to enroll <u>now</u> because waiting can result in higher premiums. I do not support cold calling and I wholeheartedly admit that I am not a fan of aggressive telemarketing agents. They give honest, hard-working Medicare agents a bad name.

Factor #4: Door-to-Door Sales

If you thought door-to-door sales were a thing of the past, you are wrong. There has been a revival of door-to-door sales in the Medicare insurance industry. I often meet with people who tell me that someone showed up on their doorstep attempting to give them information or schedule an appointment. I don't know your opinion about door-to-door sales, but I think it is intrusive and potentially dangerous. Always show caution when a stranger rings your doorbell.

Factor #5: Misinformation

I know most family and friends mean well, but I cannot tell you how many times individuals have sat across from me with information about Medicare that is not true. However, the individual is convinced he/she is right because someone they knew had told them. Once this happens, it becomes harder to convince the individual of the truth. I appreciate all well-meaning family and friends, but it can also create stress and confusion.

Factor #6: Medicare Parts versus Medicare Plans

The last factor that causes Medicare stress is what I call *Parts vs. Plans*. What do I mean by this? Did you know that Original Medicare consists of two parts, Part A and Part B? However, there are two additional parts to Medicare, known as Part C and Part D. Part C identifies Medicare Advantage plans, and Part D identifies prescription drug plans. Essentially, Medicare consists of four parts.

Now, let's create some confusion! The letters A, B, C, and D also identify Medicare supplement *plans,* which are also known as Medigap plans. So, we have Medicare Parts A, B, C, and D and then we have Medicare plans, also identified by A, B, C, and D. There are also additional letters for Medicare supplement plans such as F, G, and N.

When you receive mail with different letters such as A and B, G and N, F & D, it is easy to get confused. Confusion can lead to stress. Stress can lead to poor decisions. Does this make sense? Don't worry, I am going to explain the different *parts* and *plans* of Medicare in later sections, but for now, let's just accept that this can be a little confusing.

Moving Ahead

If you want to stop stressing and start focusing on making good Medicare decisions, here is where the rubber meets the road. At this point, I am going to lay out a plan to move you from stressed and confused to clear and confident. To move in this direction, you will need guidance, education, and a plan of action. For the rest of this guide, I intend to accomplish all three. It will require you to put forth some effort; however, if you consider what is at stake, the results will be worth it.

So, what is at stake? Penalties for not signing up for Medicare at the right time. Excessive copays for prescriptions. Large out-of-pocket expenses for medical procedures. Lastly, your peace of mind for not being confident in your Medicare decisions. However, a lot of this can be avoided, which is why I have written this book. I want you to be prepared to manage your transition to Medicare and to make confident decisions.

Stress-Reducing Actions

Listed below are actions that will help achieve the objectives of taking charge of your Medicare transition and reducing the stress you may feel that is associated with your Medicare insurance decisions. Now, there are several actions listed below. Do not allow this to overwhelm you. Some actions will require minimal effort. Others will require a little more. You may want to read the entire book first before implementing the recommended actions. You may find that you have already completed some. I am only going to ask you to *trust the process*. Let me repeat this. **TRUST THE PROCESS**. By doing so, you will be well on your way to reducing your stress and making confident Medicare insurance decisions.

- Action #1- Sign up for the National Do Not Call Registry
- Action #2- Create a Filing System with Four Folders
- Action #3 - Avoid Online Quoting

- Action #4 - Learn about Medicare
- Action #5 – Learn about Medicare Insurance Products
- Action #6 – Select a Medicare Product
- Action #7 – Identify Plan Options Available in Your Area
- Action #8 – Locate Agent and Schedule Appointment
- Action #9 – Meet with Agent and Enroll in Plan

Action #1:
Sign up for the National Do Not Call Registry

The first step to reducing your <u>Medicare stress</u> is to **register your phone numbers with the National Do Not Call Registry**. The phone number is 1-888-382-1222. You can also go online to register at www.donotcall.gov. You may be saying, "I am already on the National Do Not Call Registry and I still receive calls." I get it. I expect this is frustrating for you; however, if you are on the registry, once insurance companies or agents have this information, they are not supposed to contact you <u>without</u> *your* permission.

I realize the excessive calls may be aggravating and intrusive; however, I am going to encourage you to use them to your advantage. I am a tremendous supporter of local agents.

Once you move into Action #8, I will share more about this. It can be difficult to identify and locate a local agent. Mainly because local agents cannot compete with the giant marketing resources of large corporations.

With that said, I have two recommendations for handling the marketing calls you will receive. The first response is simple. You can avoid answering your phone. I know many people who employ this tactic. Frankly, I do not blame them.

There is a second way to respond, which may produce more positive results for you. Answer your calls from local numbers only. Once you answer the phone and the caller identifies him/herself as a Medicare agent, ask the caller the following questions:

1. Are you a local agent?
2. Do you meet with people face-to-face or online?
3. Which companies do you represent?
4. What is your phone number?

Once you have obtained this information, tell the agents you are on the National Do Not Call Registry and ask them politely not to call back. Let agents know you will keep their information and may contact them in the future if you want their assistance. If an agent calls back after being told you are on the National Do Not Call Registry, I recommend you block that agent's phone number. Why? Because the agent is disregarding the Do Not Call rules. I encourage you to avoid unethical agents, which will only benefit you. Now, take the information you have written down and put it in the Business Reply Mail folder that I will explain in Action #2. You may need that information later.

As a warning, telemarketing agents can make a local phone number show up on your phone when they call, although the call may be coming from somewhere outside of your area or state. This practice is called spoofing, and it is a deceptive practice. If you answer a local call and the agent gives you a phone number to reach him or her that is not a local number, tell the caller you are on the National Do Not Call Registry and politely request that he/she not call back. Some telemarketer agents can be aggressive. Be firm in your resolve if you encounter this behavior.

Action #1, then, is to sign up for the Do Not Call registry. Although it may not stop all calls, you will have the ability to communicate that you are on the Do Not Call Registry, which should reduce the number of calls over time. This is your first step in the process. Now go and sign up if you have not already.

Action #2:
Create a Filing System with Four Folders

Since you have already or you will be receiving a lot of Medicare mail, the next <u>action step</u> is to **create a filing system with four different folders**. You can purchase file folders anywhere that sells office supplies. Take the four folders and give them each a separate label. Label the first folder Medicare Supplements. Label the second folder Medicare Advantage plans. Label the third folder Medicare drug plans. Label the fourth and last folder Business Reply Mail. As you receive new mail, you can identify which folder it belongs in and file it appropriately.

I know you may not have much experience with Medicare, so I am going to show you how to sort the mail you receive and file it in the appropriate folder. Once you get organized and feel confident in the process, you will be able to throw away duplicate information and keep what interests you.

Here is how to identify and sort the mail you receive. The *first folder* is for Medicare supplements (also known as Medigap plans). Medicare supplements are identified by the word *plans*. Some of the more commonly used plans are A, B, F, G, and N. When you receive mail that is labeled Medicare supplement, Medigap, Plan B, Plan F, Plan G, or Plan N, etc., place that mail in the folder labeled Medicare Supplements.

The *second folder* is for Medicare Advantage plans. Medicare Advantage plans are identified as Medicare Part C. When you see mail identified with Medicare Advantage or Part C, place it in the Medicare Advantage folder.

The third folder is for prescription drug plans. Prescription drug plans are identified as Medicare Part D. When you see mail identified as prescription drug or Part D plans, place it in the prescription drug folder.

The fourth and final folder is for Business Reply Mail. Although there are several forms of Business Reply Mail, they should be easy to recognize. First, you have local agents promoting their Medicare insurance services. Second, you may get mail attempting to entice you with offers of great or extra benefits you may be eligible for. Third, you may get mail in the form of surveys or questionnaires. The main purpose of Business Reply Mail is to elicit a response by phone or by returning a card with your contact information. I suggest throwing most of this information away unless it has a local phone number on it. If it has a local phone number, it may be useful in Action #8, contacting a local agent. Place information with a local phone number in the Business Reply Mail folder. You can place the local agent information from Action #1 in this folder as well.

Here is a word of caution about Business Reply Mail. Some companies attempt to make their documents appear as *official* documents. The primary intent is to make the document look like it was mailed from Medicare (The Centers for Medicare and Medicaid Services). Do not fall for this trick. The Centers for Medicare and Medicaid Services, the official governing body for Medicare, will NEVER send you mail attempting to entice you with alleged benefits you are not receiving.

Also, as you receive mail from insurance companies, place it in your folders and write the name of the company on the left inside of each folder. This way, when you receive more mail from the same company, you will know if it is duplicate information. If so, you can throw it away. All you do is look on the inside of the folder and see if the company is listed. There is no need to keep duplicates. Once your folders are established and you begin to recognize the different types of mail, this process will become very smooth and simple.

Action #3:
Avoid Online Quoting

The next action step is to *avoid online quoting*. Perhaps I should call this step the anti-action. I want you to be aware that every website you visit is designed to capture your personal information and identify you as a potential customer. This action may be hard to resist, and I expect some of you have already done it. The main reason to avoid seeking Medicare insurance quotes online is to prevent and/or avoid being targeted as a prospect by insurance companies, marketing organizations, and lead-generation companies.

If you go to an online quoting site, whether it is directly with an insurance company or an insurance marketing group, you will undoubtedly be asked for personal information such as name, age, address, phone number, email address, etc. If you provide any of this information, you open yourself up to a barrage of unwanted advertising and contacts either by phone or email.

Be aware that the owners of the quoting site could be a lead-generation company. If you provide your information to a lead-generation company, your information will be sold to multiple agents, who will then pursue you as a potential customer. Also, if you provide your phone number, I expect there is fine print somewhere on the website that states you agree to be contacted.

To provide a quote, the only information a company needs is your zip code, age, gender, and whether you are a smoker or non-smoker. All other information can and will be used against you. So,

I recommend that you show extreme caution about providing any personal information.

With the improvement in technology, insurance companies and marketing agencies can identify your interests based on your previous web searches. The act of going to Medicare-oriented sites will increase the possibility that you will see more ads on your computer about Medicare insurance products. Did you know that once you have gone to an online site, the next site you visit can review your browsing history and orient its marketing based on your previous searches? I find it intrusive. I expect others think it is genius. I know it may be hard to resist going online, but it can help you avoid being targeted as a prospect.

Most individuals go online to obtain quotes and compare premiums for different companies. However, if you have established your file folders from action #2 as I recommend, you can access them at any time to look at monthly premium information. For each type of product, you should be able to find all the price information you need in your folders from Action #2.

Action #4:
Learn About Medicare

The action of educating yourself about Medicare **may be the single best** way to reduce or eliminate Medicare stress. If you do not have a basic understanding of Medicare, it will be difficult for you to make a confident decision. The purpose of this section is to introduce you to the basics of Medicare, such as eligibility, enrollment, and Original Medicare Parts A and B. This section does not cover every nuance or possible scenario you could experience; however, it will provide you with the essential information you need to know.

What Is Medicare?

Medicare is health insurance provided by the United States government. The U. S. Centers for Medicare and Medicaid Services (CMS) oversee the program known as **Original Medicare**. Medicare covers both inpatient and outpatient services. Inpatient services include both traditional hospitalizations and rehabilitation services. Outpatient services include doctor visits, MRIs, chemotherapy, and preventive services such as flu shots, etc. This list is not complete; however, you can be sure that your common and necessary medical services will be covered. If you want a complete list of services covered by Medicare, see Section 2 of the 2022 *Medicare and You* document published annually by The U. S. Centers for Medicare and Medicaid Services.

Medicare Eligibility

You become eligible for Medicare upon reaching the age of sixty-five. However, other situations would allow you to enroll in Medicare before reaching the age of sixty-five. If you were to develop End-Stage Renal Disease (ESRD) or Lou Gehrig's Disease, for example, you would become eligible for Medicare enrollment. Also, if the Social Security Administration determines that you have become disabled, you could enroll in Medicare after a twenty-four-month waiting period. Although, the primary qualifier for enrolling in Medicare is reaching the age of sixty-five, enrolling in Medicare before the age of sixty-five is usually the result of an illness or injury.

How to Sign Up for Medicare

You sign up for Medicare through the **Social Security Administration**. There are three options for you to complete your initial enrollment. The first option requires you to physically make a trip to your local Social Security office and sign up. The second option is for you to go online through the Social Security Administration website. The web address is https://www.ssa.gov/benefits/retirement/. You can create a _My Social Security_ account and sign up for Medicare Parts A and B online. The third option is to contact the Social Security Administration by phone at 1-800-772-1213.

If you are receiving Social Security or Railroad Retirement benefits at the time you turn sixty-five, you will automatically be enrolled in Medicare. Normally you would receive your Medicare card approximately three months _before_ the month you turn sixty-five. If you are receiving Social Security benefits and do not receive your Medicare card a month before you turn sixty-five, contact the Social Security Administration.

When to Sign Up for Medicare

If you are turning sixty-five and are _not_ covered by an employer insurance plan or receiving Social Security benefits, you will have a seven-month time frame to enroll in Medicare. These seven months are known as your *Initial Enrollment Period* or IEP. The Initial Enrollment Period begins three months before the month you turn sixty-five and ends three months after the month you turn sixty-five. As an example, if your birthday month is in April, your Initial Enrollment Period would begin on January 1 and end on July 31.

As a word of caution, if you enroll in Medicare during the first three months of your IEP, your benefits will start the first day of your birthday month. If you enroll during your birthday month, your benefits will start the first day of the next month. If, however, you wait to enroll in Medicare during the last three months, you will have a two to three-month delay before your benefits start.

Example:
Initial Enrollment Period (7 months) with an April birthday month

January	February	March	April	May	June	July
Month 1	Month 2	Month 3	Month 4 (Birthday Month)	Month 5	Month 6	Month 7

The month of Enrollment	Effective Date
January	April 1
February	April 1
March	April 1
April (sixty-fifth birthday month)	May 1
May	July 1
June	September 1
July	Oct 1

What If You Miss Your Initial Enrollment Period?

If you miss your Initial Enrollment Period and are not covered by an employer insurance plan, you have an additional enrollment period to sign up for Medicare. Your opportunity to enroll is called the **General Enrollment Period**. The General Enrollment Period runs from January 1 through March 31. If you enroll during this time, your Medicare benefits would *not begin* until July 1 of that year. Also, there is a good chance you will incur financial penalties since you did not sign up for Part B during your Initial Enrollment Period.

What If You Want to Keep Your Employer Insurance?

If you want to continue working past the age of sixty-five and maintain your employer insurance, doing so is perfectly acceptable. The employer plan, however, must be considered creditable coverage. If your employer plan is considered creditable coverage, you would not incur penalties when you sign up for Medicare once you leave your employer insurance plan. Your Human Resource and/or Benefits departments should know if your employer plan is considered creditable coverage.

Upon your retirement and transition from your employer insurance plan, you will have a Special Enrollment Period that allows you to sign up for Medicare. This Special Enrollment Period begins at whichever comes earlier, the loss of employment or the loss of employer insurance. This Special Enrollment Period lasts for eight months.

Employee Insurance and Medicare Part B

In the past, when individuals reached the age of sixty-five and wanted to continue working and maintain their employer insurance plans, they would be advised to enroll in Medicare Part A and defer Part B until retirement. That advice was good when employer plans were straight HMO or PPO plans. However, employer insurance plans have evolved, and many companies now offer *high-deductible* plans with Health Savings Accounts. If your employer insurance plan is a high-deductible plan with a Health Savings Account and you are enrolled in Medicare Part A or B, you would not be eligible to make contributions to your Health Savings Account.

However, if you have a spouse who is covered by your employer plan who is enrolled in Medicare A or B, you *will* be able to contribute to the HSA. If you are receiving Social Security or Railroad Retirement Board benefits, you have no choice but to maintain enrollment in at least Part A, which could affect your decisions if you are still employed and enrolled in a high-deductible plan.

Avoiding Penalties

For a few simple reasons, you need to know when and where to sign up for Medicare. First, you want to make sure you have health insurance. Second, if you do not sign up for Medicare at the appropriate time, you can incur monetary penalties. Medicare penalties are primarily associated with Medicare Parts B and D. If you incur Medicare penalties, they are permanent and will remain in effect while you are enrolled. You could also incur a penalty for Part A of Medicare if you do not qualify for premium-free Part A.

Medicare Enrollment Review

1. The primary qualifier for Medicare is reaching the age of sixty-five.
2. Individuals under the age of sixty-five can qualify for Medicare through a disability or certain illnesses, such as End-Stage Renal Disease or ALS.
3. Individuals sign up for Medicare through the Social Security Administration either online, over the phone, or at a local office.
4. The Initial Enrollment Period (IEP) for individuals turning sixty-five is seven months surrounding the beneficiary's birthday month.
5. Medicare-eligible individuals do not have to enroll in Medicare at the age of sixty-five if they are covered by a creditable insurance plan through their employer or spouse's employer.
6. Once an individual older than sixty-five leaves an employer plan, he/she will be able to enroll in Medicare through a Special Enrollment Period without incurring penalties.

Original Medicare (Parts A & B)

In this section, I am going to discuss Medicare Parts A and B, commonly known as **_Original Medicare_**. You must have a basic understanding of Original Medicare. Why? Because your eligibility and enrollment in Original Medicare is the gateway to enrolling in other Medicare insurance products such as Medicare supplements (Medigap plans), Medicare Advantage plans, and prescription drug plans. The purpose of this section is to help you understand the different aspects of Original Medicare, which include benefits, monthly premiums, and out-of-pocket costs (deductibles, co-pays, and coinsurance amounts). To reduce your Medicare stress and make confident Medicare insurance decisions, you must have a basic understanding of this information.

Original Medicare Card

The card shown below is an example of an Original Medicare card. The card will have your name, Medicare number, and parts of Medicare (A and B) that are effective. Remember, once you enroll in Medicare, the effective dates will always be on the first day of the month. For example, if you enroll in Medicare to begin during the month you turn sixty-five, it will begin on the first day of your birthday month. There is one exception. If your birthday is on the first day of the month, your benefits will start on the first day of the previous month.

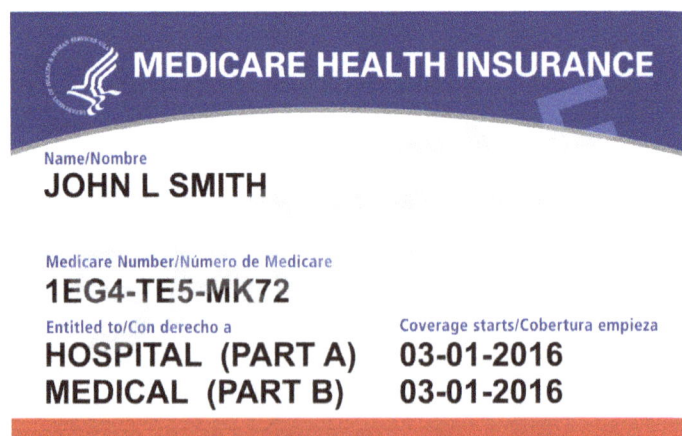

Original Medicare Part A: Coverage, Costs, and Copays

The primary coverage for Original Medicare Part A is for inpatient hospitalization and rehabilitation services. It also covers some outpatient services such as hospice and home healthcare. However, the primary coverage is for inpatient services.

Most likely, you will *not* have a premium for Part A. You qualify for premium-free Part A if you have worked a total of forty quarters (ten years) in which you paid Medicare taxes, as verified by the Social Security Administration. If you have not worked forty quarters, you can qualify for premium-free Part A through your current or former spouse's Social Security work history.

If you do not qualify for premium-free Part A, you can enroll in Part A but will have to pay a monthly premium. The amount of your premium will depend on your work history. If you have fewer than thirty working quarters in which you paid Medicare taxes, your Part B premium will be $499 per month. If you had thirty to thirty-nine working quarters, your monthly premium will be $274. These premiums are based on 2022 Medicare rate information and may change in the future.

Part A does not cover 100 percent of your medical costs. You will have Part A deductibles and co-pays. If you are admitted to the hospital while enrolled in Part A, you will have a $1,556 deductible for your hospital stay. This deductible amount is _not_ an annual deductible. The hospital deductible is applied for each benefit period. A hospital benefit period begins when you enter the hospital and ends once you have been discharged from the hospital for sixty days. After you have been discharged for sixty days, beginning on day sixty-one, a new benefit period begins and creates a new $1,556 deductible for hospital re-admissions.

Part A also has co-pays; however, Part A co-pays only apply to long-term hospital or rehabilitation stays. If you were hospitalized for sixty days, as of day sixty-one, you begin to incur a daily co-pay of $389. If the hospitalization continues beyond ninety days, your daily co-pay increases to $778 per day from day ninety-one. If you incur a hospital stay greater than 150 days during the same calendar year, you then are responsible for 100 percent of the hospital charges beginning on day 151. Yes, that could be a little scary, but later in the book, we will discuss insurance products designed to cover these types of expenses.

Additional Part A co-pays occur if you have a long-term inpatient rehabilitation stay. Your daily co-pays would begin on day twenty-one. The daily co-pay amount is $194.50. If your inpatient rehabilitation lasts longer than one hundred days, you are responsible for 100 percent of the costs beginning on day 101. Remember, for Part A inpatient hospitalizations or rehabilitation stays, your daily co-pays occur only if your admissions are extended in nature.

Original Medicare Part B: Coverage, Costs, and Copays

Original Medicare Part B covers outpatient services such as primary care physicians and specialists, MRI's, CT scans, durable medical equipment, and chemotherapy treatments. Part B also covers preventive services such as annual wellness exams, mammograms, colonoscopies, flu shots, and more. To see a complete list of items covered, review the *Medicare and You* guidebook referred to earlier. Remember, the primary coverage for Original Medicare Part B is *outpatient services*.

Part B *has* a monthly premium. The base monthly premium for Medicare Part B is $170.10. If your income is above certain levels, the Part B premium could be higher. If you are single and your income has been above $91,000, or if you are married and your income has been above $182,000, the Part B monthly premium may include an adjustment. The adjustment to the base premium of $170.10 is known as the Income Related Monthly Adjustment Amount or IRMAA.

The Social Security Administration looks at your tax records to determine your Part B premium. If you were going to enroll in Medicare in 2022, the Social Security Administration would look at your 2020 tax information, which is essentially a two-year lookback. Unfortunately, your Part B premium could reach as high as $578.30 per month if your income exceeds certain thresholds.

I am consistently asked if the IRMAA amount will be reduced in the future if your income decreases, which it normally does once someone retires. The answer is yes; however, I advise you to take the initiative to contact the Social Security office to ensure it is reduced accordingly. It could be me, but I am not going to rely on Uncle Sam to make that adjustment automatically.

If you are receiving Social Security Benefits or Railroad Retirement Board benefits, your Part B premium will be deducted from your monthly benefit check. If, however, you are not receiving Social Security or Railroad Retirement Board benefits, you will have to pay the monthly premium by another method. You can write a quarterly check or establish monthly drafts from bank accounts or credit cards, for example.

Part B has an *annual* deductible. For 2022 the annual deductible is $233. The first time each year you access your Part B benefits for outpatient services, you are responsible for the deductible. After the $233 deductible is paid, Medicare Part B covers 80 percent of all additional approved charges. *The remaining 20 percent of the bill is your responsibility.* There is no cap or limit to your 20 percent liability. Depending on your medical needs, 20 percent of certain costs could create significant financial liabilities. The twenty percent liability encourages individuals to enroll in Medicare insurance products such as Medicare supplements (Medigap plans) and Medicare Advantage plans, which provide financial protection from high out-of-pocket expenses.

What Is Not Covered by Original Medicare Parts A and B?

As you might expect, Original Medicare Parts A and B do not cover every type of medical service. Here are some items that are not covered:

- Routine vision or dental services
- Cosmetic surgery or massage therapy
- Hearing aids

- Long-term care (nursing home care)
- Medical treatments outside of the United States
- Prescription medications

This is not a complete list. However, it does give you an idea about services you may need to purchase additional insurance policies to cover, such as dental or vision. Perhaps the most important items not covered by Original Medicare Parts A and B are prescription medications. Prescription medications are covered under Part D of Medicare.

Financial Risks of Original Medicare

As you can see from the preceding information, Original Medicare has the potential for creating large liabilities under certain situations. In my opinion, the three most common financial risks you face with Original Medicare are (1) the Part A hospital deductible of $1,556, (2) the Part B twenty percent co-insurance, and (3) the lack of prescription drug coverage. This is where Medicare insurance products assist you. I will cover Medicare insurance products in the next section, which is Action Step #5.

Medicare A and B Section Review

1. Original Medicare consists of two parts (Part A and Part B).
2. Part A is usually premium-free.
3. Part B has a monthly premium starting at $170.10. Higher-income individuals can incur an IRMAA that will increase their monthly premium.
4. Part A primarily covers inpatient hospitalizations and rehabilitation services.
5. Part B primarily covers outpatient services, such as doctor visits and preventive care.
6. Part A has a hospital deductible of $1,556 per benefit period and additional co-pays for long-term hospital and rehabilitation stays.

7. Part B has an annual deductible of $233 and then a coinsurance amount of 20 percent.
8. Original Medicare does not cover prescription medications; however, it does cover medications for chemotherapy or other infusion-type treatments under Part B.

Action #5:
Learn about Medicare Insurance Products

Now that you have learned about Original Medicare, it is time to learn about the different types of Medicare insurance products that are available. These products are offered and administered by private insurance companies. The purpose of these products is to provide financial protection and benefits that are not offered by Original Medicare. Knowing some products cover the Part A hospital deductible and Part B co-insurance may relieve some of your stress, so here we go into Action #5.

The primary Medicare insurance products offered by private insurance companies are *Medicare Supplements (Medigap plans), prescription drug plans (Part D,) and Medicare Advantage plans (Part C)*. I am also going to discuss *indemnity plans*. Indemnity plans are usually combined with Medicare Advantage plans as a way of reducing financial risk. A solid understanding of these products will be essential for you to make confident Medicare decisions.

Medicare Supplements

Medicare Supplements, also known as Medigap plans, *are designed to cover deductibles and co-pays that Original Medicare does not*. Medicare supplements are identified by letters such as A, B, C, F, G, and N. Medicare supplements are a terrific product to combine with Original Medicare, because they eliminate or minimize financial risks related to medical expenses and provide tremendous flexibility in choosing medical providers. In my opinion, if you want to create the most protection from out-of-pocket costs and have the flexibility to pursue medical care wherever Medicare is accepted, a Medicare supplement is *the* choice to consider. However, you will pay an additional monthly premium for this coverage and flexibility.

Standardized Plans

Each Medicare supplement plan, such as A, B, C, F, G, etc., is standardized. This means that all plans identified by the same letter are required to offer the same benefits. For example, if two companies, X and Y, offer a Plan G supplement, the benefits offered by each company will be the *same*. The only difference will be the premium each company charges.

It is worth mentioning that some companies offer additional benefits or discounted services if you enroll in their supplement plans. These are separate from the standard benefits for each plan. For example, some companies offer benefits such as gym memberships or hearing aid discounts. When you are attempting to decide among companies, it is important to evaluate not only the plan premiums but also the additional benefits provided by the company.

Benefit Structures

Each Medicare supplement plan has a different benefit structure. As an example, an F Plan supplement will cover the Part A hospital deductible of $1,556 and Part B deductible of $233. It also covers the 20 percent Part B co-insurance. The G plan supplement will cover the Part A deductible and 20 percent Part B co-insurance. It will not, however, cover the Part B deductible of $233.

Since each plan has a different benefit structure, make sure your agent explains all the benefits of the plan you select. Also, you should know that if you are turning sixty-five after January 1, 2020, you will not be eligible to enroll in an F Plan supplement. My primary recommendation for Medicare supplements is the G Plan. It provides the maximum benefits that a Medicare supplement can offer at this time for someone turning sixty-five after January 1, 2020.

Medicare Supplement Premiums

All Medicare supplement plans have monthly premiums. As you would expect, the plans offering the most benefits will have the highest premiums. For example, a G plan supplement will have a higher monthly premium than an N plan supplement, because the G plan provides more benefits.

The monthly premium will be based on the plan you select (A, B, C, F, G, N, etc.) and the geographic area of the country in which you live. The monthly premium will also consider your age, gender, and tobacco use. Most likely every company will have different rates. Compare at least two or three companies before making a final decision. You want to ensure you are paying a competitive rate and getting the benefits you desire.

When selecting a Medicare supplement, the monthly premium is always a factor to consider. Many individuals select a specific supplement based on premiums alone. Other people select plans based on their familiarity with the company offering the plan. **Just remember that premiums for every company will increase**, so it is a good idea to ask the agent about the history of rate increases for the plans you are considering.

Eliminating Financial Risk

With a good Medicare supplement, you eliminate the risk of high medical bills, even for long-term hospital and rehabilitation stays. Original Medicare will cover the first ninety days of a hospital stay. After those ninety days are used during a calendar year, Original Medicare will provide sixty additional days, which are identified as "lifetime reserve" days. Medicare supplements will cover an additional 365 days in the hospital beyond the lifetime reserve days, so long-term hospital stays should not be a concern for someone enrolled in Original Medicare who purchases a Medicare supplement plan.

Practical Application

When an individual enrolls in a Medicare supplement, Original Medicare is the **_primary insurance._** The Medicare supplement policy follows the lead of Original Medicare. If Medicare approves and pays the medical claim, then the Medicare supplement company will pay its obligation consistent with the plan selected. If Medicare does not approve and pay the claim, the supplement company will not pay. The supplement company follows the lead of Medicare.

Also, when you enroll in a Medicare supplement, unless you have prescription coverage through another source, you will need to enroll in a Part D prescription drug plan. If you enroll in a prescription drug plan, you will essentially have three premiums every month: Medicare Part B, Medicare supplement, and prescription drug plan. Under this combination, you will have higher premiums than for other options, but you will have the lowest risk for out-of-pocket costs for medical care.

National Coverage

Another positive aspect of purchasing a Medicare supplement is the *national* coverage it provides. Medicare supplements are accepted anywhere in the United States that Original Medicare is accepted; therefore, you can go to any physician or hospital that accepts Medicare, and the supplement will be accepted.

Some Medicare supplements do not provide national coverage. This type of supplement is known as a **Select** supplement. A **Select** supplement may require you to use specific hospitals or facilities for medical care. Make sure you understand whether the supplement you choose is a traditional supplement that offers national coverage or whether it is a *select* supplement that may have restrictions for hospitals or other facilities.

Important Questions

Can I change my Medicare supplement once I am enrolled in a plan? Yes, for the most part, you can change your Medicare supplement whenever you would like; however, there is one caveat. Once your Part B becomes effective, you will have a six-month period during which you can enroll in any supplement of your choice without answering health underwriting questions. Once this initial six-month period ends, most companies require an applicant to go through medical underwriting. This means that if you have high-risk health issues, the private insurance company has the discretion to decline your application.

Will my Medicare Supplement premiums increase? Yes, most plans will have an annual premium increase. It is reasonable to expect a 3 percent to 5 percent rate increase each year, but that is not a guarantee. The rate increases will vary by company.

Medicare Supplement Review

1. Medicare Supplements are identified by Plans such as A, B, C, F, G, N, etc.
2. Medicare Supplements are offered and administered by private insurance companies.
3. To enroll in a Medicare Supplement, you must be enrolled in Original Medicare Parts A and B.
4. If enrolled in a Medicare Supplement, Original Medicare will be your primary medical insurance. The supplement will cover co-pays and deductibles that are not covered by Original Medicare as defined by the plan benefits.
5. Medicare Supplements eliminate variable costs for standard medical expenses.
6. Most Medicare Supplements have coverage nationally. **Select** supplements may have some restrictions.

Part D (Prescription Drug Plans)

Medicare prescription drug plans are identified as Part D. Part D plans cover medications your primary care doctor or specialist prescribes for you. As an example, daily medications for high blood pressure, diabetes, high cholesterol, etc., would be covered by Part D plans. These are medications you would have filled at your local pharmacy.

All Part D plans function under a similar model. Under this model or framework, each medication is placed in a specific tier and your co-pays will be based on that tier. Each plan also has four specific phases: the deductible phase, the co-pay or coinsurance phase, the coverage gap (donut hole) phase, and the catastrophic phase.

It is important to emphasize that prescription drug costs may create the most financial risk to you, as a Medicare beneficiary. Why? Because prescription medications vary from person to person. You may take two generics that are low in cost. In that case, you will probably have low co-pays for your medications. Your friend or spouse, however, may take eight medications with four generics and four brand-name medications. This will create higher prescription drug costs. *The main objective in selecting a prescription drug plan is to find the plan that covers your medications at the lowest overall cost.*

How to Obtain Part D Coverage

There are two basic ways you can obtain Medicare Part D coverage. First, you can enroll in what is known as a *stand-alone* prescription drug plan. Stand-alone plans only cover prescription medications. They do not provide any additional benefits. Another way you can obtain prescription drug coverage is through enrollment in a Medicare Advantage plan that includes prescription drug coverage. We have not discussed Medicare Advantage plans yet; we will do that next. Regardless of how you obtain Medicare Part D coverage, the same basic model will apply. Each plan will have medication tiers and four different phases.

Medication Tiers

Part D plans categorize every medication into a specific tier. Most prescription drug plans will have five tiers; however, there are a few plans that have six tiers. See the list below for the most common drug tiers.

- Tier 1 Preferred Generics
- Tier 2 Non-preferred Generics
- Tier 3 Preferred Brand
- Tier 4 Non-preferred Brand
- Tier 5 Specialty

As you may expect, *the co-pay for each medication usually increases as the tier increases*. For example, a Tier 1 generic will have a smaller co-pay than a Tier 3 preferred brand medication. There could be an exception to this occasionally, but normally the co-pays increase as the tier increases.

Part D Phases

Each prescription drug plan will have four specific phases. The first phase is the deductible phase. The second phase is the co-pay or coinsurance phase. The third phase is the coverage gap (donut hole) phase. The last phase is the catastrophic phase. The chart below shows you the specific progression.

Exhibit: Prescription Drug Plan Phases

Phase 1	Phase 2	Phase 3	Phase 4
Deductible	*Co-pay or Co-insurance*	*Coverage Gap/ Donut Hole*	*Catastrophic Coverage*

During the **deductible phase**, you as the beneficiary will pay 100 percent of the cost of your medications up to the amount of the deductible. For 2022, the deductible for a Part D plan could be as high as $480. The amount of the deductible is set by the private insurance company offering the plan. There are Part D plans that do *not* have deductibles. Usually, Part D plans that do not have deductibles have higher monthly premiums. If the Part D plan does not have a deductible, you would begin paying the set co-pay or coinsurance amount based upon the tier of your medication.

There is another trend among Part D plans. Several plans are not applying the deductible for lower-tier medications (Tiers 1 and 2), which means that if you are taking medications listed in lower tiers, you would not have to pay the deductible. Instead, you would pay the standard co-pay amount.

For plans that have a deductible, once you have paid the deductible amount, you will move into the second phase. The second phase is known as the **co-pay or coinsurance** phase. During this phase, you will pay the co-pay or coinsurance amount based on the medication tier.

Examples of Part D Co-pays/Coinsurance:

- Tier 1 Preferred Generic $5
- Tier 2 Non-preferred Generic $15
- Tier 3 Preferred Brand $45
- Tier 4 Non-preferred Brand $100
- Tier 5 Specialty 30% co-insurance

The third phase of Part D plans is known as the **Coverage Gap**. The more common street name for this phase is called the **donut hole**. You move into the Coverage Gap once the retail costs of your medications reach $4,430. Until that point, you have not been paying the retail amount. You have been paying co-pays based on the medication tier. The move into the Coverage Gap is based on the retail cost listed by the pharmacy. Those who reach the Coverage Gap are usually taking a higher-cost medication, which is usually listed in a higher tier.

Once you move into the Coverage Gap, the standard co-pay or coinsurance amounts you have been paying are no longer applied.

During the Coverage Gap, you will pay 25 percent of the cost of each medication, regardless of which tier your medication is listed. This change has the potential to raise your costs for every medication.

The fourth and final phase of Medicare Part D plans is called the **Catastrophic** phase. Once you enter the Catastrophic phase, you start paying about 5 percent of the cost of your medications. This is distinctly *lower* than the 25 percent you would pay during the **Coverage Gap** phase, but normally you would have spent several thousand dollars before you move into the Catastrophic phase.

Monthly Premiums

Every Part D *stand-alone* plan will have a monthly premium. The monthly premium could range in price from about $7 per month to more than $100 per month. As you might expect, the plan with the higher premium usually covers a larger formulary of medications and has lower deductibles. Insurance companies have some discretion in designing the plans they offer and what monthly premiums they charge.

If your previous income puts you into the position of having an Income Related Monthly Adjustment for Medicare Part B, you will also have an adjustment for your Part D premium. The adjustment amount could range from $12.40 to $77.90 per month.

Deductible or No Deductible

The maximum deductible a prescription drug plan can include is $480 per year (for 2022), but not all plans have deductibles. Usually, higher premium plans reduce or eliminate deductibles. When I say higher premium plans, I am referring to plans with monthly premiums greater than $50, but this amount can vary from state to state. As always, make sure you compare at least two or three plans before making a final decision. If you select the wrong plan, it could cost you hundreds, if not thousands of dollars per year.

Formularies

Every prescription drug plan has a specific formulary. A formulary is the list of medications covered by each plan. As you may expect, the plan with a $7 premium will usually *not* cover the same number of medications as a plan with a $75 monthly premium. Here is something you need to know: All drug plans are required to cover at least two medications in *every* drug category, so even lower-cost plans cover a significant number of medications.

Preferred or Standard Pharmacies

Every prescription drug plan will have preferred and standard pharmacies. If you use the preferred pharmacies, you will usually pay a lower co-pay. If you use a standard pharmacy, you will pay a higher co-pay. Make sure you know the preferred pharmacies in your plan. This has the potential to save you money.

Important Questions

What happens if my medications change? Most people I work with are concerned with this question. Here are a couple of things to consider. First, every drug plan covers at least two medications in every drug category, so there may be a good chance that something in the plan's formulary will meet your need. If the specific medication your physician prescribed is not on the formulary, you have the option of requesting an exception to the formulary. I cannot guarantee the request would be granted, but it is something you can try.

Can I change my prescription drug plan? Yes, you can change your prescription drug plan every year during the Annual Enrollment Period, which runs from October 15 through December 7. During that time, preexisting conditions are not considered and you can choose from any plan that is available in your area. Also, if you have been discussing new medications with your physician, make sure you consider the potential medications in your choice of a new plan. That way if you make a change, your new medications would be covered.

Do I have to enroll in a Part D plan? The answer is no, but if you do not enroll in a Part D plan when you are first eligible, you may be subject to financial penalties if you sign up for a prescription plan at a later date.

Medicare Part D Review

1. Part D covers prescription medications.
2. Part D plans are offered and administrated by private insurance companies.
3. Part D plans usually have five tiers. Medications usually have lower co-pays in the lower tiers.
4. Co-pay amounts will change if a beneficiary goes into the Coverage Gap.
5. Premiums for prescription plans are set by each insurance company. Plans with higher premiums may eliminate deductibles.
6. Higher premium plans usually cover a larger number of brand-name drugs and have lower co-pays.
7. Always know the preferred pharmacies for each plan.
8. When selecting a prescription drug plan, always consider medications you are taking and those you have been discussing with your physician.
9. Individuals can change Part D drug plans during the Annual Enrollment Period (October 15 through December 7) without preexisting condition considerations.
10. Medicare does not require enrollment in Part D, but enrollment after initial eligibility may create a permanent financial penalty.

Medicare Advantage Plans (Part C)

Medicare Advantage Plans are identified as Medicare Part C. Insurance companies offering Medicare Advantage plans have contracted with The Centers for Medicare and Medicaid Services as a requirement to offer this type of plan. Insurance companies who offer Medicare Advantage plans have oversight from The Centers for Medicare and Medicaid Services and are required to follow specific guidelines.

Medicare Advantage plans must offer the equivalent benefits of Original Medicare Parts A and B. Therefore, the same benefits of Original Medicare will be covered by each Medicare Advantage plan. However, each plan will have a different structure for co-pays and deductibles, which is usually different than Original Medicare.

I have spoken to several people over the last few years who are hesitant to enroll in Medicare Advantage plans. The main reason is their concern about losing their Original Medicare benefits. You will not lose your Original Medicare benefits by enrolling in a Medicare Advantage plan. Enrollment in Original Medicare (Parts A and B) is a requirement for enrolling in a Medicare Advantage plan.

Once you enroll in a Medicare Advantage plan, essentially the private insurance company administers your Original Medicare Part A and B benefits. You will receive a card from the private insurance company that will be used when receiving medical services. You will *not* be able to use your Original Medicare card when receiving medical services, but since you still maintain your enrollment in Original Medicare, always keep your Original Medicare card. You may decide to return to Original Medicare in the future.

HMOs or PPOs

There are different types of Medicare Advantage plans such as Health Maintenance Organizations (HMO), Preferred Provider Organizations (PPO), Private Fee for Service Plans (PFFS), Special Needs Plans (SNP), HMO Point of Service Plans (HMO-POS), and Medicare Savings Account Plans (MSA). In this section, I am going to focus on HMO and PPO plans, primarily because they are the two most prevalent options. If you are interested in enrolling in a Medicare Advantage plan, you must understand the options available in your geographical area. The types of plans and benefits offered by each plan may and often vary from state to state and even from county to county.

Let's start with HMO plans. A Medicare Advantage HMO has a strict network of providers. You <u>must</u> stay within your network for claims to be paid by the plan. If you are enrolled in an HMO and you go out of network, *you will have to pay for the services*. In most cases, you must have an in-network primary care physician. With an HMO, some plans require a referral to see a specialist, but more and more HMO plans are eliminating this requirement. *It is important to remember that you are responsible for following the rules of the plan and will receive the maximum benefits by staying within your plan's provider network.*

A Medicare Advantage PPO also has a network of providers; however, a PPO plan allows you to seek services or treatment outside of the plan's network. Usually seeking treatment outside of the plan's network requires higher co-pays. *If you do not want to have restrictions on where you receive care and want to have a large option of providers, a PPO plan may be a better selection for you than an HMO plan.*

How Medicare Advantage Plans Function

Medicare Advantage plans provide the equivalent of Original Medicare Part A and B benefits. From a consumer's perspective, Part C plans are administered in a way that combines the characteristics of an employer health plan with Original Medicare. Medicare Advantage plans usually have a combination of established co-pays for certain services and co-insurance amounts for others.

Here is an example: If you are enrolled in a Medicare Advantage plan, you will have set co-pays for physician services such as primary care providers and specialists. The plan may require you to pay a $10 co-pay for a primary care physician visit and a $30 co-pay for a specialist visit. For other services you receive, you will have a coinsurance amount that matches Original Medicare. For example, under Original

Medicare, you would pay a 20 percent coinsurance for durable medical equipment such as wheelchairs or oxygen. The same would apply to most Medicare Advantage plans. You would also pay a 20 percent coinsurance for those services. Each Medicare Advantage plan has a list of medical services that would require you to pay a co-pay amount and a list of services that would require you to pay a co-insurance amount. You must understand how each of the benefits provided by a Medicare Advantage plan would be billed to you.

Out-of-Pocket Maximums

One benefit of enrolling in a Medicare Advantage plan instead of using Original Medicare (without additional supplemental coverage), is the requirement that each plan must have a Maximum Out-of-Pocket limit, sometimes referred to as MOOP. *Every Medicare Advantage plan has a maximum out-of-pocket limit.* A *maximum out-of-pocket* limit sets a cap or limit on the amount you *could* incur for medical costs each year, provided you stay within your network. Under Original Medicare, there is no cap on your liability, so the Part B coinsurance of 20 percent could accumulate to an unlimited amount based on the type of services you may receive.

Under a Medicare Advantage plan, you have a maximum liability each year regardless of total costs. The highest *Maximum Out-of-Pocket* amount a Medicare Advantage plan can currently establish is $6,700. Once you look at specific plans, I expect you will be able to find plans that have *lower* amounts. This amount is set by the insurance company offering the plan. You need to know that the maximum out-of-pocket limits *do not* include co-pays for prescription medications. The co-pays and coinsurance amounts credited to you each year toward the maximum out-of-pocket limits are strictly related to medical services.

Prescription Coverage or No Prescription Coverage

Medicare Advantage plans may or may not include Part D prescription drug coverage. Plans that do not cover prescription medications usually have lower premiums (in many cases no premiums at all) and lower Maximum Out-of-Pocket limits. *A plan without prescription drug coverage could be a good option if you have prescription coverage through another source, such as the Veterans Administration or a retiree health plan or if you do not take medications for personal or religious reasons.*

High-Risk Areas

If you enroll in a Medicare Advantage plan, it is not likely you would have enough co-pays or co-insurance amounts to reach your Maximum Out-of-Pocket limit for routine medical care. However, I wanted to mention higher-risk services that could move you toward that amount. The first service would be hospitalizations. Medicare Advantage plans usually have a daily hospital co-pay. This co-pay could range from an estimated $150 to $300 per day for a set number of days, usually five to seven. If you incurred a hospitalization for five days at $175 per day, the total co-pay amount would be $875. It is important to remember the daily co-pay covers all aspects of the hospitalization, which would include doctors, procedures, nursing care, etc. If you have multiple inpatient hospitalizations in one year, it could add up to significant costs.

The next service that could create large out-of-pocket expenses for you would be the use of Part B medications. Part B medications are chemotherapy or other infusion-type medications. Under most Medicare Advantage plans, chemotherapy or infusion-type treatments have a coinsurance amount of 20 percent. This figure matches the same coinsurance amount as Original Medicare, but with a Medicare Advantage plan, your liability could never exceed the *Maximum Out-of-Pocket* limit. Still, if a plan has a Maximum Out-of-Pocket limit of $5,000, that is a large amount to pay for many people.

One way to protect against high hospital and cancer treatment costs is through the use of medical indemnity plans. You can purchase a hospital or cancer indemnity plan that will protect you against these higher-risk areas. I recommend everyone who enrolls in a Medicare Advantage plan consider adding indemnity policies to protect against these higher-risk areas. I will discuss indemnity plans in more detail later in this section.

Premiums

Because you are required to maintain your enrollment in Original Medicare Parts A and B as a prerequisite for enrolling in a Medicare Advantage plan, you will always pay your Part B premium. The Medicare Advantage plan may require you to pay an additional premium. The premium amount is decided by the private insurance company offering the plan. It is common to see Medicare Advantage plans, HMOs, and PPOs that do not have additional premiums. Always understand what your total monthly premiums will be if you enroll in a Medicare Advantage plan.

Additional Benefits

Some of the attractive features of Medicare Advantage plans are the extra benefits some plans include. The extra benefits may include dental, vision, allowances to assist with over-the-counter items, and gym memberships. The extra benefits a Medicare Advantage plan offers can truly make this type of plan a well-rounded healthcare option. Medicare Advantage plans are often referred to as "all in one" plans. The additional benefits are very appealing to many individuals and often affect enrollment decisions. Remember, Original Medicare does not cover dental, vision, or over-the-counter items.

Pre-Existing Conditions

When you enroll in a Medicare Advantage plan there are no restrictions for pre-existing conditions. You can enroll and change Medicare Advantage plans regardless of any medical issues you may have incurred. Although, I would suggest that if you are working with a local agent, it might benefit you to share with the agent any special treatments or conditions you may have. This will allow the agent to provide more expertise and advice. However, Medicare agents are not supposed to ask you any health questions during a Medicare Advantage plan consultation.

Important Questions

Can I change my Medicare Advantage plan if I am not happy? Yes, you can change your Medicare Advantage plan every year during the <u>Annual Enrollment Period</u>, which runs from October 15 through December 7. Along with changing your Medicare Advantage plan during this time, you could also dis-enroll and return to Original Medicare as your primary insurance. Also, during the Open Enrollment Period (separate from the Annual Enrollment Period), which runs from January 1 through March 31, you have an opportunity to make one change to your Medicare Advantage plan. The Open Enrollment Period is relatively new to Medicare recipients, so many people are not aware they have this option. Also, there are Special Enrollment Periods that would allow you to make changes as well. An example of a Special Enrollment Period would be if you moved to a new state or if you qualify for the Extra Help program for prescriptions. Several Special Enrollment Periods would allow you to make changes. These are just a few.

Am I losing my Original Medicare? No, you are not losing your Original Medicare. As I stated previously, you must be enrolled in Original Medicare as a qualifier for enrolling in a Medicare Advantage plan. However, during the time you are enrolled in a Medicare Advantage plan, you would not be able to use your Original Medicare card for medical services. You would receive an insurance card from the private insurance company to be used during your enrollment.

Medicare Advantage plans may not be the choice for everyone, but they have the potential to provide excellent coverage and benefits under the right situation. There are usually multiple plan options available in most states. Make sure you understand the cost and benefit structures for each plan you are considering. Also, make sure you understand the provider networks (doctors and hospitals) before enrolling in any plan.

Medicare Advantage Plan Review

1. Medicare Advantage plans are offered and administered by private insurance companies.
2. Individuals who want to enroll in a Medicare Advantage plan must be enrolled in Original Medicare (Parts A and B).
3. Medicare Advantage plans usually have defined networks of providers such as doctors and hospitals. HMO plans usually have _no_ out-of-network coverage unless an exception is granted. PPO plans have a network but also provide out-of-network coverage, usually with higher co-pays.
4. All Medicare Advantage plans have a Maximum Out-of-Pocket limit for the beneficiary. Original Medicare does not.
5. Medicare Advantage plans that do not cover prescription medications usually have lower premiums, co-pays, and out-of-pocket maximums. They are also good options for individuals who can obtain prescription coverage through another source, such as the Veterans Administration or retiree medical plans or people who have no interest in taking medications.
6. Medicare Advantage plans may have an additional premium to pay along with the Part B premium.
7. Medicare Advantage plans may include additional benefits such as vision and dental.
8. Two of the high financial risk areas for Medicare Advantage plans are hospitalizations and Part B medications, such as chemotherapy.
9. Consider using indemnity plans to lower risks of high co-pay items such as hospitalizations and cancer treatments.

Indemnity Plans

Indemnity plans are not specific to Medicare. However, they are often combined with Medicare Advantage plans as a way of providing additional financial protection for out-of-pocket expenses. Indemnity plans are usually designed to cover costs and expenses related to specific medical conditions such as cancer, strokes, heart attacks, hospitalizations, etc. *I recommend that everyone enrolled in a Medicare Advantage plan consider enrolling in a cancer indemnity and/or hospital indemnity plan.* The combination of a Medicare Advantage plan with an indemnity plan can often provide a high level of support and financial protection with lower premiums than Medicare supplements (Medigap plans).

Cancer Indemnity Policy Example

If you enroll in a $5,000 lump-sum cancer indemnity plan and later receive a cancer diagnosis, the insurance company would pay you a lump sum of $5,000. This $5,000 could be used to cover medical co-pays or coinsurance amounts related to your treatments. Usually, you would want to purchase an indemnity plan that covers your Maximum Out-of-Pocket amount. So, if your Maximum Out-of-Pocket is $5,000, you will want a policy that covers at least $5,000.

Hospital Indemnity Policy Example

Most Medicare Advantage plans require you to pay a daily hospital copay for a specified number of days. A hospital indemnity plan will pay the daily co-pay amount, which reduces your out-of-pocket costs for inpatient hospital stays. So, if your Medicare Advantage plan has a hospital copay of $250 for the first five days of your hospital stay, you would want to have an indemnity plan that would reimburse you $250 for those first five days. Therefore, covering your hospital co-pay amount.

Indemnity Plan Review

1. Indemnity policies are offered by private insurance companies.
2. Indemnity policies cover specific illnesses such as cancers, heart attacks, strokes, and hospitalizations.
3. Cancer and hospitalization policies are recommended for all individuals enrolled in Medicare Advantage plans.

Action #6:
Select a Medicare Product

Now that you have learned about Medicare and the different types of Medicare products, it is time to take the next step and *select a Medicare product* that best suits your personal needs and interests. There are two main options (although not the only) that most people select to obtain their Medicare benefits. The first option is to maintain your Original Medicare benefits and add a Medicare supplement and stand-alone drug plan (if you want prescription drug coverage). The second option is to enroll in a Medicare Advantage plan, which may or may not have prescription drug coverage, depending on the plan you choose. Making this decision often creates <u>Medicare stress</u> for many people. To facilitate this process, I have created a series of questions designed to help you clarify which Medicare product may suit you best. There are two sets of questions listed below. Read and answer each question. Keep track of your answers.

Section A Questions

1. Would you like to have access to doctors or hospitals outside of the geographic area where you reside?
2. Would you pursue treatment for a medical condition anywhere in the United States if you felt like it was in your best interest?
3. Are you willing to pay a monthly premium to obtain more financial protection from out-of-pocket expenses?

4. Are you more comfortable when you can eliminate financial risk?
5. Are you willing to pay out-of-pocket or additional premiums for services that are not covered by Medicare, such as dental, hearing, and vision benefits?

Section B Questions

1. Are you comfortable working within a network of physicians or providers?
2. Are you okay with paying regular co-pays for medical services to save money on lower monthly premiums?
3. Are you willing to take some financial risks to save money on insurance premiums?
4. Are you comfortable having some financial risk if you know the risk is capped at a certain amount?
5. Do you want to have a comprehensive healthcare plan that includes additional benefits, such as dental and vision, that are not covered by Medicare, without paying an additional premium?

If you answered yes to more questions in Section A, you may be more inclined to purchase a Medicare Supplement to work alongside your Original Medicare. If you answered yes to more questions in Section B, you may be inclined to purchase a Medicare Advantage plan. At this point, you should be gaining more clarity about which option you prefer. Now it is time to identify plans available in your geographical area. This is Action #7!

Action #7:
Identify Plan Options Available in Your Area

You have learned about Medicare (Action #4). You have learned about the different types of Medicare insurance plans (Action #5). You have also considered the type of plan you are most interested in (Action #6). The next action step is to identify the Medicare plans that are available in your geographic area. For this action, I recommend that you look in two primary places. First, refer to the folders you created in Action #2. If you are not satisfied with the information from your folders, you can then search the Medicare.gov website. The purpose of this action is to create an initial target list of companies you are interested in learning more about.

There are specific reasons why I am recommending that you look at these two primary resources (your file folders and Medicare.gov). First, most companies that offer Medicare plans in your geographic area will send you information through the mail. So, if you followed Action #2, you have a good source of available plans in your folder. Second, the Medicare.gov website will list all Medicare Advantage and prescription drug plans available in your zip code. I still recommend that you avoid completing online searches because doing so will open you up to increased marketing calls and mailings. Remember, you want to reduce your Medicare stress, not add more.

Steps for Identifying Medicare Advantage Plans

1. The first step is to review your Medicare Advantage plan folder from Action #2. At this point, you have received plenty of mail from insurance carriers. Select four or five plans and write them on a piece of paper or place a check by their names on the inside of your folder if you followed my earlier instructions. This will be your <u>initial</u> target list. You can add or delete plans as you choose. You may believe you have enough information from your folder that you do not need to complete a Medicare.gov search. If you are content with your initial list, stop here. If not, continue to the next step.
2. The second step is to look up Medicare Advantage plans on Medicare.gov. Once you are online, go to Medicare.gov and follow the steps listed below.
   - Select the tab Find Plans (Find 2022 Health and Drug plans)
   - Once you select the Find Plans tab, you will be asked if you have a Medicare account or if you want to create an account. You can proceed without creating an account, but I recommend that you create an account to prevent having to re-enter information each time you return. Create an account and then follow the prompted questions. I also recommend that you enter your prescription drug information, which will allow you to see the expected drug costs per each plan.
   - After following each prompt, you will land on the page that lists all the available plans. Look to the right side of the screen. You will see a "sorting" tool. Sort your search results by "Lowest drug + premium cost." This action will sort and list the plans from the lowest premium plus medication costs to the highest premium plus medication costs.
   - You can now review the plans available in your area. While on this page, there is specific information on the

Medicare.gov website that may be of interest to you. Each of the items listed below will be found on the preview page. Look at this information for each plan. It may help guide your interest.
1. The Medicare star ratings are from one to five. Higher is better.
2. The plan premium.
3. HMO or PPO.
4. Out-of-Pocket Maximum amount.
5. Co-pays for primary care and specialist physicians.
6. Expected prescription costs.

Once you have completed steps one and two, you should have a good target list of plans, which will prepare you for Action #8.

Steps for Identifying Prescription Drug Plans

1. The first step is to review your Prescription Drug plan folder from Action #2. You have probably received plenty of mail from insurance carriers. Select four or five plans and write them on a piece of paper to make your initial target list or place a checkmark on the inside of your folder by the plans you are interested in. You might want to add or delete plans once you complete your search from step two listed below.
2. The second step is to look up prescription drug plans on Medicare.gov. This action is imperative because it shows your projected drug costs for the year. This information itself could eliminate certain plans. To accomplish this step, go to Medicare.gov and follow the steps listed below.
   - Select the tab Find Plans (Find 2022 Health and Drug plans).
   - Once you have selected the Find Plans tab, you will be asked if you have a Medicare account or if you want to create an account. You can also proceed without creating

an account, but I recommend that you create an account to prevent having to re-enter information each time you return. Create an account and then follow the prompted questions. Enter your prescription drug information, which will allow you to see your expected drug costs.

- Once you have entered your prescription drug information, you will advance to a page that lists all the available plans.
- On the right side of your screen, you will see a <u>sorting</u> tool. Sort your search results by "Lowest drug + premium cost." This action will sort and list the plans from the lowest premium plus medication costs to the highest premium plus medication costs.
- You can now review the plans available in your area. Compare the lower-cost plans with the plans you have selected from your folder and then revise your target list if necessary. For each plan listed, there is specific information you want to review. See the list below.
    1. Star Ratings from one to five. The higher the star rating the better.
    2. Premium.
    3. Estimated Drug Costs

You should now have a good target list of prescription drug plans and be prepared to move into Action #8.

Steps for Identifying Medicare Supplement Plans

When it comes to identifying Medicare Supplement plans that are available in your area, the primary source is going to be the mail you have received. However, you can look up Medicare supplements on the Medicare.gov website. Unfortunately, the site does not provide a lot of price information per company. It will show you companies offering Medicare supplements in your geographical area.

First, review your Medicare Supplement folder from Action #2. I am confident you have received an abundance of advertisements for Medicare supplements. Review your folder and pick out a few well-known companies that you recognize.

If you want to consider more company options, go to Medicare.gov and follow the steps listed below.

- Select the tab Find Plans (Find 2022 Health and Drug plans).
- Select Medicare Supplements and answer the corresponding questions.

Once you have answered the corresponding questions, you will be taken to a page that lists the available supplement plans. If you click on the tab *View Polices*, you will see companies that are offering plans in your area. You can scroll through the list and select companies you are interested in learning about. Once you have a list from your folder and Medicare website, you are ready to move on to Action #8.

Remember the lists you have created are simply a beginning point. Once you meet with an agent, he/she will most likely provide you with additional information. On many occasions, an experienced and knowledgeable agent will recommend plans you did not select.

Action #8:
Contact an Agent and Schedule an Appointment

If you have completed the previous steps, you are ready for Action #8, which is to contact an agent and schedule an appointment. As a Medicare insurance agent since 2014, I have not met with a single person who did not have questions, uncertainty, or confusion about Medicare. This compels me to recommend that you work with a knowledgeable and experienced Medicare insurance agent. If you want someone who can educate, counsel, enroll, and support you, you need an agent. In the next few paragraphs, I am going to share with you the types of agents who assist individuals with Medicare.

Agent Options

Local Independent Insurance Agent (also known as an insurance broker). The independent agent (broker) is not employed by an insurance company; however, the agent represents multiple companies. The agent will be licensed in one or more states and will live in your local geographic area. This agent usually meets with customers face to face, but most likely will have the ability to counsel individuals online or over the phone as well.

Local employed agent (also known as a career agent). This insurance agent is employed by a specific insurance company and therefore represents *one* specific company. The agent will live in your geographical area. This agent meets with customers face-to-face and can counsel individuals online or over the phone.

Local independent captive agent. This agent is not an employee of an insurance company, but the agent has signed an agreement to represent only one company for specific products, usually Medicare Advantage plans. The agent will live in your local geographical area. This agent meets with customers face-to-face and will have the ability to counsel individuals online or over the phone.

Call-center agent. The call-center agent may be employed by a specific insurance company or by a national marketing agency. If the agent is employed by an insurance company, the agent will represent only one plan. If the agent is employed by a national marketing organization, the agent usually represents multiple insurance companies. This agent works over the phone.

Telemarketing independent insurance agent (also known as an insurance broker). This agent works for himself/herself and usually represents multiple companies. The agent works over the phone and will most likely be licensed in multiple states. This agent does not meet with individuals face to face.

Agent Recommendations

When you become eligible for Medicare, you will have the opportunity to work with any of the agents listed above. The agent you choose to work with is a personal decision. However, this is an important decision. Therefore, I am going to provide you with my recommendations.

My _first and primary_ agent recommendation is the **local independent agent** (also known as a broker). First, a local agent will be able to meet with you face-to-face. It is usually much easier to understand Medicare information when you are sitting with someone who can answer your questions and provide handheld information for you to review. Since the agent represents multiple companies, he or she should not pressure you to choose a particular company, but instead, help you identify the company that best fits your needs.

A good local agent will understand how plans are accepted in the local medical community, especially the Medicare Advantage plans.

The agent is invested in your community and will want to maintain a good reputation for service because the agent will want future referrals.

The last reason I recommend an independent local agent is that your insurance needs are going to change over time. If you have a relationship with a local agent, you will be able to contact the agent with questions and sit down to discuss your needs as they change. If you have a relationship with a local agent, all you need to do is pick up the phone to schedule an appointment.

My <u>second</u> recommendation is to work with a **local employed agent**. Because these agents represent one company, they should understand their company plans very well. The drawback is that these agents represent ***only*** one company, so their main goal is to enroll you in *their* company plans. If you work with a local employed agent, I recommend that you speak with at least two or three different companies.

You also have the option of working with call-center agents or independent telemarketing agents. Although working with a telemarketing agent could be functional, it is not what I recommend. My concern is that you would not have support or possibly any contact with the agent once you have enrolled in a Medicare plan. I hope you will consider my recommendations before making your decision. However, the decision is ultimately yours.

Finding Agents

Now that I have provided you with my agent recommendations, I will give you some direction on how to find and contact a local agent. If you do not have an agent selected, here are some ways to locate the agents I have recommended.

Some local agents have offices; others work out of their homes. You may find a few listed in the phone book. Most independent local agents I know rely on word of mouth and their reputation for obtaining new clients. So, if you perform an online search, the majority of options you find will be large insurance companies or national marketing agencies (call centers), not local agents. Local agents cannot spend the money to compete online with large insurance companies or marketing organizations, so internet searches will often prove unsuccessful.

Here are tips for finding an independent local agent:

1. If you followed my recommendation from Action #1 and answered some of your local calls, you can pull out that list and review it.
2. Review your Business Reply Mail folder and see if any have local contact numbers.
3. Ask friends or family members if they have worked with a local agent.
4. Ask your primary care doctor if they have any recommendations.

If you cannot locate a local independent agent (broker), it is easy to locate a local employed agent. All you need to do is contact the insurance company directly and say you want to meet with an agent face-to-face. The insurance company will provide your information to one of its employed or captive agents, who will then contact you to schedule an appointment.

If you want to work with a telemarketing agent, all you need to do is call one of the numbers from a commercial or answer your phone when a telemarketer calls you. There will be no shortage of incoming telemarketer calls.

You now have your target list of plans and are ready to meet with an agent or agents. Depending on the plans the agent represents, you may have to meet with a few different agents to cover your interests. Do not worry; it will be worth your time.

Action #9:
Meet with Agent and Enroll in a Plan

You are coming down the home stretch. **It is time to meet with an agent or agents and enroll in a plan that you choose.** This last step may take a few hours of your time. It is common to meet with an agent more than once. The first meeting will often be to discuss your Medicare questions and the various insurance options. The second meeting is usually to enroll. This schedule will vary based on your interest and preparedness. You may be ready to enroll on the first visit.

Let's talk about enrolling in a Medicare plan. If you have met with a local agent who has answered your questions and assisted you through this process, I encourage you to use that agent to enroll. Local independent agents are compensated only through enrollments and spend countless hours educating and preparing individuals to make good Medicare decisions.

The other options are to enroll through call centers or telemarketing agents, mail-in applications, and even online. Frankly, I do not recommend any of these options. However, I know as a matter of convenience, these options are often used. If you are uncertain or confused about Medicare, enrolling through these options creates a higher risk of making mistakes, which could be financially and emotionally costly over time.

Conclusion

Now, if you have followed my recommended actions, you will have completed a lot of work. Look at the list below. Congratulations on the effort you have made!

- Action #1- Sign up for the National Do Not Call Registry
- Action #2- Create a Filing System with Four Folders
- Action #3 - Avoid Online Quoting
- Action #4 - Learn about Medicare
- Action #5 – Learn about Medicare Insurance Products
- Action #6 – Select a Medicare Product
- Action #7 – Identify Plan Options Available in Your Area
- Action #8 – Locate Agent and Schedule Appointment
- Action #9 – Meet with Agent and Enroll in Plan

The process you went through may have seemed long and involved, but the process of transitioning to Medicare continues to confuse and overwhelm most people. I hope that after reading this book and following the actions I recommend; your Medicare stress will be reduced and you feel more confident in your Medicare insurance decisions. I wish you the best. May you have many happy and fulfilling years as a Medicare recipient.

www.ingramcontent.com/pod-product-compliance
Lightning Source LLC
Chambersburg PA
CBHW040518220526
45473CB00012B/2904